Endless JOY Journal

She's VIP 31 Day Process to Actualize Your Dreams and Thrive!

TeQuita A. White-Muhammed

To My Dear Friend Benton, may every life's joy always see you through
~ TeQuita

This Journal Belongs To:

_____

Endless JOY *Journal*

Your {4 Week / 31 Day} Guided Journal designed to help you Ignite your VISION and Thrive!

Dedication

This journal is dedicated to Jessie Mae Jones, my Lady Bug. The one who showed me infinite love and JOY through it all. The one who encouraged me to dream and never stop soaring! And to my 3T's {Terra, Telley, and Tash}, you are my inspiration to build a legacy......no matter what!!

Purpose of this Journal

She's VIP JOY Journal focuses on asking empowering questions daily over the course of 31 days. By asking the right questions you can incite your unconscious mind to supply you the answers you need to operate in your JOY filled purpose. Each of us is connected to and worthy of infinite JOY. Over the next 31 days, I hope to help you spark a small flame; a flame that will grow into the JOYously passionate life you envision.

How to Use this Journal

Use this Journal as a vision and creation guide to get to what you desire in your heart space. Your current reality is moving toward what you envisage. For some this may be getting back to what you started many years ago. For others, it may be getting to where you've always wanted to be. Embrace your inner guiding source, and start to set intentional goals directed by JOY and purpose.

Utilize the Daily Empowering questions as a base line to build out your daily affirmations and afformations. Start with writing out your goals as you are instructed and guided in the Daily envisioning exercises. Set aside at least 30 minutes a day to write. Completing the JOY journey will strengthen your vision and power your passion.

Give yourself permission to welcome in JOY each day. Most importantly, allow yourself to be blessed and to be a blessing to others. I hope you enJOY this JOY Journal as you move closer to your happiest, best life!

Personal Declaration

My future is up to me; if it's to be, it's up to me. I, _____, have the power to go after what I envisage and what I desire in my heart. I, _____, am dedicated to developing the attitude of never giving up on my dreams and goals. I, _____, am committed to changing the thought patterns, habits, and routines that have presented obstacles along my journey to bliss. I have everything I need to live a life filled with bliss and I boldly envisage a beautiful future created by design! I am, unapologetically, a dream actualizer and I dwell in infinite JOY!!

Sign: _____

Date: _____

Table of Contents

Circle of JOY Wheel

This exercise will help you identify which areas of your life need a JOY jolt. Allowing yourself the time to give attention to these areas will create more harmony in your life. The circle has 12 sections. Each section can be further broken down into subsections as you build out your daily JOY.

For the purpose of this exercise, you will rate the categories from 1 to 10. With 10 representing ultimate JOY and happiness. This will give you a clear visual of any areas you may need to allow special attention. Over the next 31 days, think of these categories as you complete your daily entries.

You will complete this exercise again at the end of your 31-day journey to see if your wheel becomes more balanced. Remember to count it ALL JOY and embrace the process!

Areas to Envisage Change in Your Life: JOY Assessment on a scale of 1-10

Category	JOY Rating
1. Health & Physical Wellness	_____
2. Emotional Intelligence	_____
3. Relationships	_____
4. Spirituality	_____
5. Finances	_____
6. Professional Career	_____
7. Educational Skill Sets	_____
8. Natural Gifts and Talent	_____
9. Ideation and Creativity	_____
10. Home Environment	_____
11. Social and Community Connections	_____
12. Self Actualization	_____

Endless JOY *Daily Guide*

She's VIP Daily Baseline Affirmation: You will create a personal belief statement to deliberately guide your forethought. Make it personal, action driven, accurate, and realistic. It should positively call to your emotions and indicate achievement. These daily statements will become your personal Affirmations.

Example: I thrive in my daily breathing exercises because it helps me feel centered, healthy, strong, well, and energized.

Breakdown:
- "I" makes it personal
- "thrive" is action driven
- "daily" is accurate and realistic
- "feel centered, healthy etc." calls to positive emotion and achievement

She's VIP Daily Empowering Afformation Question: Asking the right question can incite your unconscious mind to supply you the right answer. Creating Afformations (empowering questions) based on your Affirmations will help you become a successful, high-performing individual, who WINS frequently. These Afformation questions will allow you to come up with immediate, right NOW, present tense, answers designed to move your life forward and create endless JOY!

She's VIP Daily Envisage Exercise: You will complete a daily exercise to spark a flame and bring clarity regarding what consistent actions you can take to move you into your JOY space, each day.

She's VIP Bonus TIP: Every other day you will journey through a bonus activity to 10X your Vision!!

Week 1

> Bliss is the place where you unleash your amazing power, embrace the process, and thrive in JOY!
>
> *TeQuita A. White-Muhammed*

This Week's Intentions

_____

_____

_____

_____

_____

_____

_____

_____

_____

_____

_____

_____

_____

_____

_____

_____

_____

Day 1

She's VIP Daily Baseline Affirmation:
I am Poised in Purpose.

_____

_____

She's VIP Daily Empowering Afformation Question:
Why do I have a positive expectancy to be poised in purpose?

_____

_____

_____

_____

_____

_____

_____

_____

_____

_____

Day 1 Envisage Exercise:

Take time to imagine all day - Envision the life you want in mental and physical pictures as well as tangible objects.

From this envisioning exercise, write down 10 big dreams and desires that emerged throughout the day. These ideas and dreams will be the foundation to bringing you JOY as you seek to actualize them.

31 Days to Actualize Your Dream and Thrive

Day 2

She's VIP Daily Baseline Affirmation:
I am Happiness.

_____

_____

She's VIP Daily Empowering Afformation Question:
Why do I live such an amazingly happy and JOY filled life? What little things bring me JOY daily?

_____

_____

_____

_____

_____

_____

_____

_____

_____

Day 2 Envisage Exercise:

Identify your JOY Jolts - this includes what makes you smile, feel warm inside, and make you laugh. Humor invigorates the soul!

List 10 experiences that bring you happiness. Look for ways to increase these types of occurrences in your life daily.

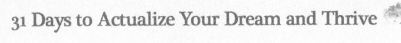

BONUS She's VIP Tip 1

Champion Your Ideal!

You may ask: How do you champion your idea?

First you must have clarity and focus. What problem does your idea solve and who is the ideal beneficiary of your solution? In order to identify these individuals, adequate market research is required.

Secondly, you must believe whole-heartedly in your idea. You are the one with the vision, so guard it carefully. Be excited and boldly radical about the success of your idea. It takes others five-to-seven exposures to your solution before they will buy in and/or adopt the idea.

Lastly, seek support in promoting your idea. This can be in the form of monetary resources, focus groups, and the bartering of your solution in exchange for services or products from someone who can provide you with testimonials as you build experience and results.

Always be open! EnJOY and embrace the process... this is how we Win!

Action Item:

Write one step you took this week to champion your idea.

_____

_____

_____

_____

_____

_____

_____

_____

_____

_____

_____

_____

_____

_____

_____

_____

31 Days to Actualize Your Dream and Thrive

Day 3

She's VIP Daily Baseline Affirmation:
I am Nimble and Agile.

_____

_____

She's VIP Daily Empowering Afformation Question:
What allows me to have an excellent free-flowing memory? Why is it
so easy for me to flow and recall clearly?

_____

_____

_____

_____

_____

_____

_____

_____

_____

Day 3 Envisage Exercise:
Change is an inevitable part of our lives. It is necessary to be open to embracing the process of change. Are you aware when change is on the horizon? Do you ever expect or anticipate it?

- Identify the changes you sense happening around you.
- Identify how the changes make you feel. Are they welcomed or unwelcomed?
- Identify ways you can adapt to unwelcomed changes with minimum impact to your JOY.

_____

_____

_____

_____

_____

_____

_____

_____

_____

_____

_____

31 Days to Actualize Your Dream and Thrive

Day 4

She's VIP Daily Baseline Affirmation:
I am Forgiven.

_____

_____

She's VIP Daily Empowering Afformation Question:
Why do I afford myself and others the grace to forgive? Why am I free and unstuck in my spirit? How do I grow my forgiveness muscle daily? Why do I easily overcome hurt and disappointment?

_____

_____

_____

_____

_____

_____

_____

_____

_____

_____

Day 4 Envisage Exercise:

Identify where you are—your current state, what's working for you and what's not working in all the major areas of your life. Refer to the JOY Wheel for major areas to consider.

Decide who and what you should keep in your life.
- Identify what you need to add.
- Identify what you need to modify.
- Identify what you need to discard.

_____

_____

_____

_____

_____

_____

_____

_____

_____

BONUS She's VIP Tip 2

Know your Why!

What is the positive outcome of achieving your goal and who will it benefit? Does it get you one step closer to a larger or more long-term goal?

Understanding and clearly defining the goal and objectives will enable you to push through days and situations that may challenge reaching the mark.

The WHY also provides you with a push and reason that goes beyond you. This type of motivation is always rewarding.

Action Item:

Clearly define the reason why you want to achieve three short-term goals each quarter.

_____

_____

_____

_____

_____

_____

_____

_____

_____

_____

_____

_____

_____

_____

31 Days to Actualize Your Dream and Thrive

Day 5

She's VIP Daily Baseline Affirmation:
I am full of Ideas.

_____

_____

She's VIP Daily Empowering Afformation Question:
Why am I an idea generator? How do I open myself to an endless flow of ideas and downloads? When I receive new ideas, how do I act to develop them?

_____

_____

_____

_____

_____

_____

_____

_____

_____

Day 5 Envisage Exercise:
Determine where you desire to be in the next 12 months in three major areas of your life.

Write down what you envision for your future state in those areas.

List questions that will bring the vision to reality and help you get one step closer to your place of solace.

_____

_____

_____

_____

_____

_____

_____

_____

_____

_____

31 Days to Actualize Your Dream and Thrive

She's VIP Daily Baseline Affirmation:
I am a Value Adder and Solution Provider.

_____

_____

She's VIP Daily Empowering Afformation Question:
Why do I diligently find solutions to challenges daily? Why do I seek and give value continuously?

_____

_____

_____

_____

_____

_____

_____

_____

_____

_____

Day 6 Envisage Exercise:
Start the discovery process for the future state you envision. What are your happiness factors?

Allow yourself time to work through this exercise. Today is a great day to create a mind map.

Write down everything you consider to be requirements for reaching the vision you desire.

_____

_____

_____

_____

_____

_____

_____

_____

_____

BONUS **She's VIP** Tip 3

When creating your goal, break it down into manageable time-bound steps.

Creating goals that are S.M.A.R.T. will enable you to maintain a clear focus on what you will achieve. Without focus, you could be caught in a spiral of efforts that are not productive. The entire reason for setting the goal is to get to the end result in the most efficient manner. Below is an outline of the S.M.A.R.T. goal acronym. Use it as an outline for setting manageable goals. The goals should be written and executed as follows:

S   specific, significant, stretching
M   measurable, meaningful, motivational
A   agreed upon, attainable, achievable, acceptable, action-oriented
R   realistic, relevant, reasonable, rewarding, results-oriented
T   time-based, time-bound, timely, tangible, trackable

Action Item:

Select one of the goals you set for 2019 and apply the SMART Goal framework.

Remember to post your goal with your accountability support system!

_____

_____

_____

_____

_____

_____

_____

_____

_____

_____

_____

_____

_____

_____

_____

_____

31 Days to Actualize Your Dream and Thrive

Day 7

She's VIP Daily Baseline Affirmation:
I am a Currency Generator.

_____

_____

She's VIP Daily Empowering Afformation Question:
Why do I choose prosperity over poverty? How do I generate a
constant flow of currency through relational connections and idea
generation and implementation?

_____

_____

_____

_____

_____

_____

_____

_____

Day 7 Envisage Exercise:
Prioritize what's required to reach the goals you have written.

Determine if the items you have listed are essential for your happiness or if they are simply nice to have.

If the items are simply nice to have, consider going for the gold. Remember this is your dream, so make it BIG - no holds barred.

_____

_____

_____

_____

_____

_____

_____

_____

_____

_____

31 Days to Actualize Your Dream and Thrive

Weekly Reflections

Endless
JOY
Journal

31 Days to Actualize Your Dream and Thrive

Week 2

"

Vision is the guiding force that shapes our lives.

TeQuita A. White-Muhammed

"

This Week's Intentions

Day 8

She's VIP Daily Baseline Affirmation:
I am a Winner, Action Taker, and Decision Maker.

_____

_____

She's VIP Daily Empowering Afformation Question:
What makes me immune to fear and any possibility of failure?

_____

_____

_____

_____

_____

_____

_____

_____

_____

_____

Day 8 Envisage Exercise:
Always note your next steps by creating a roadmap. This roadmap will by your guiding plan to reach your dreams.

Today, take time to review your prioritized goals and determine which one you will set to accomplish over the next 3, 6, and 12 months.

Next, determine which ones you will focus on for the next 2, 5, and 7 years. Joy is continuous, so you want to create a long-term strategy for your life.

_____

_____

_____

_____

_____

_____

_____

_____

_____

_____

31 Days to Actualize Your Dream and Thrive

BONUS She's VIP Tip 4

Set aside a dedicated time to work on your goal daily. Consistent intentional actions performed over a dedicated period of time will enable you to accomplish your goal.

Action Item:
Determine a specific time to work on your goals daily. Write it down and commit to completing at least one vision-focused task during that time each day.

Remember to factor in time to rejuvenate.

_____

_____

_____

_____

_____

_____

_____

_____

_____

_____

_____

_____

_____

31 Days to Actualize Your Dream and Thrive

Day 9

She's VIP Daily Baseline Affirmation:
I am a Process Optimizer.

_____

_____

She's VIP Daily Empowering Afformation Question:
What processes do I create to optimize my potential, thoughts, ideas, and goals? Why do I implement my processes and refine them when needed?

_____

_____

_____

_____

_____

_____

_____

_____

Day 9 Envisage Exercise:

Joy is a deliberate action. It starts with setting defined goals.

Today, break down your goals into tractable, tactical action steps.

Identify your resource limitations and how you increase your capacity and currency flow to manifest your dreams.

_____

_____

_____

_____

_____

_____

_____

_____

_____

_____

_____

31 Days to Actualize Your Dream and Thrive

Day 10

She's VIP Daily Baseline Affirmation:
I am Thankful.

_____

_____

She's VIP Daily Empowering Afformation Question:
Why do I maintain a positive, prayerful, and thankful attitude daily?

_____

_____

_____

_____

_____

_____

_____

_____

_____

_____

_____

Day 10 Envisage Exercise:
Celebrate milestones and small achievements. Today just celebrate you for being consistent and reaching Day 10 of the journey.

Write down what you are proud of yourself for doing and being.

Commit it to your memory for continuous support in reaching your joy space. These memories will become your happiness factors and will fuel you when you feel like things are getting heavy.

_____

_____

_____

_____

_____

_____

_____

_____

_____

_____

31 Days to Actualize Your Dream and Thrive

BONUS She's VIP Tip 5

Categorize and prioritize your goal.

In order to assure peak performance with regard to your goals, make sure they align with your key areas for improvement from your JOY Wheel.

Five pillars you can establish as categories in which to focus your goals are:

1. Personal Development
2. Business / Professional Development
3. Spiritual Development
4. Wellness
5. Finance

You can set specific S.M.A.R.T. goals for each category, then prioritize them in order of importance.

One way to prioritize the goals is to establish timeframes for completion:
- Short-Term   2 weeks to 90 days
- Intermediate   6 months to 12 months
- Long-Term   12 months to 24 months
- Roadmap Items   more than 2 years, but less than 7 years

By breaking down the goals into categories and priorities, you can experience continuous progress. This will help you stay on track because you will have consistent wins, which limits discouragement.

Action Item:
Establish two goals for each of your pillars, then prioritize them ranging from short-term to long-term.

_____

_____

_____

_____

_____

_____

_____

_____

_____

_____

_____

_____

_____

31 Days to Actualize Your Dream and Thrive

She's VIP Daily Baseline Affirmation:
I am Victorious.

She's VIP Daily Empowering Afformation Question:
Why do I refuse to live a defeated life? Why do I choose to have peace and boundaries that facilitate victory in my life? Why do I have victory over any defective mentality? Why am I victorious over vices, bad habits, addictions, deep hurts, and struggles?

Day 11 Envisage Exercise:

Securing your place of peace is part of the joy journey. This calls for the ability to identify and mitigate your risk; especially the risk of giving up.

Today you will create a strategy for not giving up. Identify reserves, controls, and stop-gates that will help you stay focused on your goals. One way is to create your "Quad A" team.

Enlist your Angel, Advocate, Ambassador, and Accountability Partner. This can be two or more individuals.

1. Angel - Will invest time and resources in helping you achieve your goals.
2. Advocate - Will make connections and open doors for you that you cannot open.
3. Ambassador - Will sing your praises and support you in championing your ideas, products, and services.
4. Accountability Partner - Will help you stay on task and commit to what you say you will do.

_____

_____

_____

_____

_____

31 Days to Actualize Your Dream and Thrive

_____

_____

_____

_____

_____

_____

_____

_____

_____

_____

_____

_____

_____

_____

_____

_____

_____

_____

_____

_____

_____

31 Days to Actualize Your Dream and Thrive

Day 12

She's VIP Daily Baseline Affirmation:
I am Abundance.

_____

_____

She's VIP Daily Empowering Afformation Question:
Why am I abundantly happy?

_____

_____

_____

_____

_____

_____

_____

_____

_____

Day 12 Envisage Exercise:
Choosing Joy does not come without obstacles and hurdles. But you can prepare for challenges by developing healthy coping skills. Prepare for the unknown by creating provisions and contingencies for the constraints.

Research and list tools you will use to maintain your joy during stressful times. Here are a few mechanisms to start with:
1. Listen to soothing music.
2. Perform breathing exercises.
3. Eat plenty of fruit and vegetables, and exercise regularly.
4. Face the issue and get professional help when needed.

_____

_____

_____

_____

_____

_____

_____

_____

31 Days to Actualize Your Dream and Thrive

BONUS She's VIP Tip 6

Determine a method for tracking your goals.

You can use manual or electronic tracking tools.

Examples of manual tools include journals, goal posters, and goal boards.

Examples of electronic tracking tools include Excel spreadsheets or tracking applications.

A few goal tracking applications:
- Google Keep (Free)
- Simplenote (Free)
- Apple Notes
- TiddlyWiki (Free)
- Microsoft OneNote
- Google Drive
- Dropbox Paper
- Box Notes

Action Item:

Decide on a method for tracking your goals and enter the three goals along with the action items and tasks you set for each of the goals identified.

_____

_____

_____

_____

_____

_____

_____

_____

_____

_____

_____

_____

_____

_____

_____

_____

31 Days to Actualize Your Dream and Thrive

She's VIP Daily Baseline Affirmation:
I am Intentional.

_____

_____

She's VIP Daily Empowering Afformation Question:
Why am I intentional with my speech and thoughts? Why do I speak clearly, calmly, and make positive contributions that benefit me and those I impact?

_____

_____

_____

_____

_____

_____

_____

_____

_____

Day 13 Envisage Exercise:
Taking on too much at work or home can impact your Joy negatively, but the ability to be agile and flexible within your work-life balance structure will help solidify your joy factors.

Benefits to being agile and flexible include increased creativity, productivity, and improved well-being, with a sense of happiness and work-life satisfaction.

Research and list tools you will use to maintain your Joy when your schedule becomes demanding. Here are a few techniques to start with:
1. Look for opportunities to work remotely.
2. Be open to continuous improvement.
3. Enlist help from others to complete tasks.

_____

_____

_____

_____

_____

_____

_____

_____

_____

31 Days to Actualize Your Dream and Thrive

She's VIP Daily Baseline Affirmation:
I am a Creator and an Innovator.

_____

_____

She's VIP Daily Empowering Afformation Question:
How do I sharpen my creative skills and flow in a space of innovation daily?

_____

_____

_____

_____

_____

_____

_____

_____

_____

Day 14 Envisage Exercise:
Allow your creative flow to propel you forward and own your power!
Prayer, meditation, and daily quiet time allows the creativity to
overflow endlessly.

Design your daily routine to nurture your creative flow. Outline the
activities, time of day, and length of time you will commit to being still
and centered. Make it a priority for your peace of mind!

_____

_____

_____

_____

_____

_____

_____

_____

_____

_____

31 Days to Actualize Your Dream and Thrive

BONUS She's VIP Tip 7

Research your goal and understand the level of effort involved in attaining your goal.

Determining the complexity of your goal is critical to the success of achieving it. As you identify the dynamics of the goal, you can properly plan the estimated timeline for completing and actualizing it. You want to set realistic expectations as not to be overwhelmed by the efforts and requirements to reach it. This tip will also assist you in prioritizing the goal.

Action Item:

Determine the complexity of the three goals you set for the second quarter of 2019. Are they simple or complex? What are the requirements necessary to actualize them?

_____

_____

_____

_____

_____

_____

_____

_____

_____

_____

_____

_____

_____

_____

31 Days to Actualize Your Dream and Thrive

Weekly Reflections

Weekly Achievements

_____

_____

_____

_____

_____

_____

_____

_____

_____

_____

_____

_____

_____

_____

_____

_____

_____

_____

_____

_____

_____

_____

_____

31 Days to Actualize Your Dream and Thrive

Week 3

> Life, at its essence, is change.
> In fact, every day of our life means
> change because every day you are a
> different person from the day before.

Noah St. John

This Week's Intentions

Day 15

She's VIP Daily Baseline Affirmation:
I am filled with Gratitude.

_____

_____

She's VIP Daily Empowering Afformation Question:
Why am I so grateful and filled with gratitude daily?

_____

_____

_____

_____

_____

_____

_____

_____

_____

_____

Day 15 Envisage Exercise:
When you share your dreams and goals, know that there will be
impacts and push back. Keep striving until you're thriving.

List ways you will tune out the noise and stay focused on achieving
your dreams.

_____

_____

_____

_____

_____

_____

_____

_____

_____

_____

_____

_____

31 Days to Actualize Your Dream and Thrive

She's VIP Daily Baseline Affirmation:
I am Brilliant and Shine Bright as the rarest Red Diamond.

_____

_____

She's VIP Daily Empowering Afformation Question:
What about me is uniquely made? How can I let my light shine fully
and operate in my uniqueness daily?

_____

_____

_____

_____

_____

_____

_____

_____

_____

_____

Day 16 Envisage Exercise:
Sometimes it takes a hybrid approach to get to your dream. Be open to non-traditional paths along the way to your happy place. A little bit of this and a little bit of that can be blended to create your own formula and methodology.

Think of "outside the box" ideas you have for reaching your dreams and write them down.

_____

_____

_____

_____

_____

_____

_____

_____

_____

_____

_____

31 Days to Actualize Your Dream and Thrive

BONUS She's VIP Tip 8

Celebrate your micro WINS!!!

Every small achievement leads to BIG success, so always reward yourself for each new level that you meet in the process of attaining and actualizing your goal.

Action Item:
You are halfway through the goal of completing the 31-day JOY Journal. Go out and celebrate. I love cake pops and flower shops... so I say, smell a rose today! But no matter what, celebrate you TODAY, *your way*!

_____

_____

_____

_____

_____

_____

_____

_____

_____

_____

_____

_____

31 Days to Actualize Your Dream and Thrive

She's VIP Daily Baseline Affirmation:
I am Positioned on Purpose.

_____

_____

She's VIP Daily Empowering Afformation Question:
In what way am I positioned on purpose?

_____

_____

_____

_____

_____

_____

_____

_____

_____

Day 17 Envisage Exercise:

Seek feedback from a wise council. Advisors are wonderful assets, but you must choose your council wisely. Always follow your Sprit Voice when seeking out your advisors.

Identify what type of advisor(s) you will need to help you reach your full potential and Endless Joy.

1. Fitness Trainer
2. Life Coach
3. Professional Mentor
4. Spiritual Confidant

_____

_____

_____

_____

_____

_____

_____

_____

_____

_____

31 Days to Actualize Your Dream and Thrive

She's VIP Daily Baseline Affirmation:
I am an Inspirer and Leader.

_____

_____

She's VIP Daily Empowering Afformation Question:
Why do I live a life of inspiration and leadership? Who do I get the
opportunity to help guide, lead, and inspire?

_____

_____

_____

_____

_____

_____

_____

_____

_____

Day 18 Envisage Exercise:
We talked about accountability partners early on in the 31-day process. Accountability partners want to see you as a VIP!

Today, reach out to your accountability partner and schedule your meeting time for the next 90 days. Give them a high-level list of three goals you will achieve in the next quarter. And get them to commit to helping you reach your goals.

_____

_____

_____

_____

_____

_____

_____

_____

_____

_____

_____

_____

31 Days to Actualize Your Dream and Thrive

BONUS She's VIP Tip 9

Be aware that there is a distiction between your Desire and the goal. Get clear on what you desire and then set how and when you will achieve the desired outcome... (this is the goal portion).

Action Item:

Revisit your desires from Day 1 and set three goals to help you reach each desire.

_____

_____

_____

_____

_____

_____

_____

_____

_____

_____

_____

_____

_____

_____

31 Days to Actualize Your Dream and Thrive

Day 19

She's VIP Daily Baseline Affirmation:
I am Walking in Purpose.

_____

_____

She's VIP Daily Empowering Afformation Question:
Why do I have pride in walking in purpose?

_____

_____

_____

_____

_____

_____

_____

_____

_____

_____

Day 19 Envisage Exercise:
It is important to revisit your vision daily. Immerse yourself in every facet of what you see coming into existence. Be dedicated to making the vision a reality and manage the activities required to reach the goals by setting up time for the daily review.

_____

_____

_____

_____

_____

_____

_____

_____

_____

_____

_____

31 Days to Actualize Your Dream and Thrive

Day 20

She's VIP Daily Baseline Affirmation:
I am a Believer.

_____

_____

She's VIP Daily Empowering Afformation Question:
Why do I conduct my life and actions by faith? Why do I hold on to my values and beliefs? Why do I release those items that do not serve me or increase my faith?

_____

_____

_____

_____

_____

_____

_____

_____

Day 20 Envisage Exercise:
Be committed 100% with a joyful zest and childlike belief.

List 50 traits that you believe, that you KNOW, are wonderful about yourself. Draw from your positive attributes, including your morals, beliefs, convictions, talents, and likes.

_____

_____

_____

_____

_____

_____

_____

_____

_____

_____

_____

_____

_____

31 Days to Actualize Your Dream and Thrive

BONUS She's VIP Tip 10

The Goal is Actualized when you deem it a MUST. It's only when a firm decision is taken, and a no-matter-what attitude is adopted, that you will push forward through all obstacles and distractions to reach the mark.

Action Item:
Write a no-matter-what letter to yourself today. Encourage yourself to never give up. List all the special characteristics that will give you the strength, courage, tenacity, and audacity to keep going!

_____

_____

_____

_____

_____

_____

_____

_____

_____

_____

_____

_____

_____

31 Days to Actualize Your Dream and Thrive

Day **21**

She's VIP Daily Baseline Affirmation:
I am a Dream Actualizer.

_____

_____

She's VIP Daily Empowering Afformation Question:
What actions do I take to fully manifest my dreams daily? Why am I
great at making daily decisions that bring me closer to actualizing my
dreams?

_____

_____

_____

_____

_____

_____

_____

_____

_____

Day 21 Envisage Exercise:

Your vision is bigger than you. It is meant to serve the world and by default you will be served and elevated to your joyful place as well.

Clearly define the following:
- The WHY, the reason you are creating your dream.
- The WHO, those that will benefit from your vision.

_____

_____

_____

_____

_____

_____

_____

_____

_____

_____

_____

31 Days to Actualize Your Dream and Thrive

Weekly Reflections

Endless
JOY
Journal

31 Days to Actualize Your Dream and Thrive

Endle
JOY
Journ

Week 4

> Success is not the key to happiness.
> Happiness is the key to success.
> If you love what you are doing,
> you will be successful.

Herman Cain

This Week's Intentions

Day **22**

She's VIP Daily Baseline Affirmation:
I am Healthy.

_____

_____

She's VIP Daily Empowering Afformation Question:
Why am I happy that I am healthy and energetic? Why do I deserve to treat my body with love and respect?

_____

_____

_____

_____

_____

_____

_____

_____

_____

Day 22 Envisage Exercise:

Relaxation time and self-care are essential for your happiness. Today I want you to focus on the activities that relax you.

Go out or stay in and do something that relaxes you. Afterwards, write down how the experience has impacted your state of joy.

---

31 Days to Actualize Your Dream and Thrive

BONUS She's VIP Tip 11

Be prepared to tweak your goal and course correct along the way. It's imperative that you are visiting your goals daily. Often revisions, modifications, and enhancements will result from being fully engaged and connected with your vision. Remember, perfection is achieved over time. You will make the adjustments as you go. Just continue to show up and diligently work it step by step.

There is a quote by Bob Proctor that says:
"What you hold in your head, you can hold in your hand."

This means that as you focus on and complete the actions necessary to reach the goal, it is guaranteed to Actualize!

Action Item:

Share with your accountability partner how you determine when a goal needs to be tweaked and what steps you take to revise your goals when course correction is required.

Remember to Keep Marching forward and Enjoy the journey!

---

31 Days to Actualize Your Dream and Thrive

She's VIP Daily Baseline Affirmation:
I am created by the Greatest for Greatness.

_____

_____

She's VIP Daily Empowering Afformation Question:
Why am I aware that the power in me emulates from the Source greater than me, and radiates for greatness in this world? What am I aware of that will come to be through me?

_____

_____

_____

_____

_____

_____

_____

_____

_____

Day 23 Envisage Exercise:
Stay connected to the Almighty Source. We win when the Creator guides our steps. Visioning occurs when we are in relationship and take time to listen for guidance daily.

Start by praying: "I center myself and recognize the Infinite, Divine —I am one in it ...unconditional love—step into that space absolutely knowing I'm unconditionally loved sit in the silence—let it relax and center me..." Rev. Dr. Michael Beckwith

Begin to ask from the Source the following questions on a daily basis:
1. What is God's highest vision for my life, my relationship, my next step, my perfect idea, (and whatever you are visioning for with JOY)?
2. Is there anything new or in addition to what I currently know, or any other information that I need to have revealed at this exact time?

_____

_____

_____

_____

_____

_____

_____

31 Days to Actualize Your Dream and Thrive

Endless
JOY
Journal

_____

_____

_____

_____

_____

_____

_____

_____

_____

_____

_____

_____

_____

_____

_____

_____

_____

_____

_____

_____

_____

_____

_____

31 Days to Actualize Your Dream and Thrive

Day 24

She's VIP Daily Baseline Affirmation:
I am Humble.

_____

_____

She's VIP Daily Empowering Afformation Question:
What keeps me operating in a space of humility and humbleness?

_____

_____

_____

_____

_____

_____

_____

_____

_____

_____

Day 24 Envisage Exercise:

Write what brought you JOY today and list what you are grateful for in your life. Establish your gratitude routine. Here are a few suggestions:

1. Pray in every situation - comfortable and uncomfortable.
2. Send those you are grateful for "Gratitude Notes" letters, text messages, emails, or postcards.
3. Perform a random act of kindness.

_____

_____

_____

_____

_____

_____

_____

_____

_____

_____

_____

_____

31 Days to Actualize Your Dream and Thrive

BONUS She's VIP Tip 12

Listen to promptings in your spirit. This is your guiding source leading you to your endless joy. Allow the visioning to emerge.

Action Item:
List the various downloads you have received over the years and then meditate on them. This will boost your creativity and move you to action.

_____

_____

_____

_____

_____

_____

_____

_____

_____

_____

_____

_____

_____

31 Days to Actualize Your Dream and Thrive

Day 25

She's VIP Daily Baseline Affirmation:
I am full of Energy and Life.

_____

_____

She's VIP Daily Empowering Afformation Question:
What energizes me and fuels my drive to live a full life?

_____

_____

_____

_____

_____

_____

_____

_____

_____

_____

Endless
JOY
Journal

Day 25 Envisage Exercise:
Draw knowledge, wisdom, and understanding from lessons learned during the process to fuel you forward expeditiously.

Document what you have experienced during this 31-day process to date. What has come up for you? Comfortable and uncomfortable feelings, thoughts, and emotions?

_____

_____

_____

_____

_____

_____

_____

_____

_____

_____

_____

_____

_____

31 Days to Actualize Your Dream and Thrive

Day 26

She's VIP Daily Baseline Affirmation:
I am a Joy Catalyst.

_____

_____

She's VIP Daily Empowering Afformation Question:
Why do I choose to share and stimulate joy in myself and others?

_____

_____

_____

_____

_____

_____

_____

_____

_____

_____

_____

Day 26 Envisage Exercise:

Inclusion is key to maintaining Harmony with your family and closest friends. Engage your family to assist you in building your dreams and joyful place.

Today, carve out special time with your immediate family. Share, at a high level, three of the dreams and goals you have identified during this 31-day process.

---

31 Days to Actualize Your Dream and Thrive

BONUS She's VIP Tip 13

Build and nurture relationships that will support you in reaching your goals. Remember, it's the Power of Who.

Action Item:

Identify individuals in your life who fall into the following roles and send them a thank you note for being part of your support circle.

1. Who's your cheerleader?
2. Who's your accountability partner?
3. Who's your prayer partner?
4. Who's your trusted confidant?
5. Who makes you laugh?
6. Who do you look up to?
7. Who's your biggest supporter?
8. Who gives you energy?

Remember, they are here to elevate and support you in being your best!

_____

_____

_____

_____

_____

_____

_____

31 Days to Actualize Your Dream and Thrive

Day 27

She's VIP Daily Baseline Affirmation:
I am Consistent.

_____

_____

She's VIP Daily Empowering Afformation Question:
What allows me to be consistent and have well organized plans?

_____

_____

_____

_____

_____

_____

_____

_____

_____

_____

Day 27 Envisage Exercise:

Allow yourself the space to grow through this process. Be patient and kind to yourself while holding yourself accountable.

List what has been useful for you during this process. What has surprised you in a good way and what do you need to pay special attention to in developing the life you envision?

_____

_____

_____

_____

_____

_____

_____

_____

_____

_____

_____

31 Days to Actualize Your Dream and Thrive

Day 28

She's VIP Daily Baseline Affirmation:
I am a Resource Connector.

_____

_____

She's VIP Daily Empowering Afformation Question:
Why do I enjoy connecting people and resources to those seeking
them?

_____

_____

_____

_____

_____

_____

_____

_____

_____

Day 28 Envisage Exercise:

Be open to partnership and collaboration—you are not alone in designing and developing your dream.

Identify the type of partnerships you need to establish in reaching your dreams. Who are you currently aligned with, and are those collaborations productive? Create a guideline for vetting future collaborations.

31 Days to Actualize Your Dream and Thrive

BONUS She's VIP Tip 14

The most important step in actualizing your goal is to start it. The plan for achieving your ultimate vision doesn't have to be perfect, but it does have to be a working plan.

Action Item:

Develop a working plan for the three goals you set out to achieve in Quarter Two of 2019. Include the following in your plan:

1. Revenue source
2. Spending needs
3. Timeframe for completion
4. Your level of effort for creation
5. Engagement level from others for creation
6. Other resources needed for creation

Keep pushing to new horizons, VIP!

_____

_____

_____

_____

_____

_____

_____

_____

_____

31 Days to Actualize Your Dream and Thrive

Weekly Reflections

Endless
JOY
Journal

31 Days to Actualize Your Dream and Thrive

Final Week

Find out where the joy resides,
and give it a voice far beyond singing.
For to miss the joy is to miss it all.

Robert Louis Stevenson

This Week's Intentions

She's VIP Daily Baseline Affirmation:
I am Dedicated to Continuous Growth; personal, relational, professional, and spiritual.

_____

_____

She's VIP Daily Empowering Afformation Question:
Why do I choose to face each day with deliberate and passionate actions that stimulate growth in every area of my life?

_____

_____

_____

_____

_____

_____

_____

_____

_____

Day 29 Envisage Exercise:
Implementation and execution are essential to reaching your goals. Always stay in motion with consistent actions. Embrace the new reality you have and are continuously creating.

Identify the financial resources required to continue to build your dreams. Create a revenue plan and a spending plan for your dream.

_____

_____

_____

_____

_____

_____

_____

_____

_____

_____

_____

_____

31 Days to Actualize Your Dream and Thrive

Day 30

She's VIP Daily Baseline Affirmation:
I am flowing in my Gifts of inspiration and dream actualizing.

_____

_____

She's VIP Daily Empowering Afformation Question:
Why am I brave enough to share my gifts with the world and make my dreams a reality?

_____

_____

_____

_____

_____

_____

_____

_____

_____

_____

Day 30 Envisage Exercise:

Once actualized, keep it new and innovative; continue building. Keep what works, tweak what needs to be modified, and release what no longer serves a purpose and is complete. Remember, it's a continuous process!

Take the JOY Wheel Assessment again today. Look at what is working and the areas that have improved. Identify what is working and what needs special attention.

_____

_____

_____

_____

_____

_____

_____

_____

_____

31 Days to Actualize Your Dream and Thrive

BONUS She's VIP Tip 15

Design and Embrace the Process

Socrates says, "The secret of change is to focus all your energy, not fighting the old, but on building the new."

Each goal you Actualize brings you one step closer to the new dream you envision for yourself. The decision, plan, and actions you take from the process is how you will attain your heart's desire.

You must be creative and flexible as you flow through the process. Although hurdles and obstacles may arise, remain positive and agile in your pursuit to reach the goal.

A daily routine and laser focus, partnered with a no-matter-what attitude will propel you into abundant living.

Stay Encouraged, Embrace the Process and keep Actualizing Your Goals and Dreams...

Thanks for playing full out Visionaries, Champions, and Jewels!

Love ya and continue the success!

- TeQuita

Action Item:

Document the top three new strategies that you developed over the past 30 days. Be committed 100% to implementing the strategies going forward and actualize your dreams.

_____

_____

_____

_____

_____

_____

_____

_____

_____

_____

_____

_____

_____

_____

_____

_____

31 Days to Actualize Your Dream and Thrive

She's VIP Daily Baseline Affirmation:
I AM LOVED and I AM LOVE!

_____

_____

She's VIP Daily Empowering Afformation Question:
Why do I choose love over hate in all situations? Why do I allow
others to feel love in my presence daily? Why do others feel the love I
genuinely share? Why do I celebrate love and living life fully?

_____

_____

_____

_____

_____

_____

_____

_____

_____

Day 31 Envisage Exercise:
Celebrate again and again, and again CELEBRATE! You MADE IT!
Go out and celebrate you!

Stay consistent and NEVER EVER GIVE UP. You were designed for
greatness and you are more than worthy of JOY and happiness.

By completing this 31 Day JOY Journal journey, you have created a
blueprint for achieving Joy in your life. Now it's up to you to continue
to actualize your dreams.

You are of excellence and this is just the beginning of your joy-filled
life. GO... LIVE, CREATE, IMPACT, and THRIVE in Endless JOY!

_____

_____

_____

_____

_____

_____

_____

_____

31 Days to Actualize Your Dream and Thrive

Weekly Reflections

Endless
JOY
Journal

_____

_____

_____

_____

_____

_____

_____

_____

_____

_____

_____

_____

_____

_____

_____

_____

_____

_____

_____

_____

_____

31 Days to Actualize Your Dream and Thrive

Circle of JOY Wheel

YES, YES, and YESSSSS!!! Now that you have completed the 31-day process to start fully living a life focused on JOY, you can revisit your Circle of JOY Wheel. At the start of this journey, you identified areas of your life that required special attention. Now let's evaluate how your daily actions have moved the needle in each of these categories.

Areas to Envisage Change in Your Life: JOY Assessment on a scale of 1-10

Category	JOY Rating
1. Health & Physical Wellness	_____
2. Emotional Intelligence	_____
3. Relationships	_____
4. Spirituality	_____
5. Finances	_____
6. Professional Career	_____
7. Educational Skill Sets	_____
8. Natural Gifts and Talent	_____
9. Ideation and Creativity	_____
10. Home Environment	_____
11. Social and Community Connections	_____
12. Self Actualization	_____

Continued JOY Wish List

Now that you have completed the post assessment and identified areas you wish to continue to elevate with JOY, create a wish list to keep those desires in your VISION. What will it take to actualize them? How will you continue to make those parts of your life juicier and more exciting? On the lines below, list the top three areas that you will commit to focus on this quarter. Keep in mind, this is a journey and the past 31 days were a jump start to ignite your passion, to be intentional, and to follow through for YOU!

- _____

- _____

- _____

Closing
Quote

I've come to believe that each of us
has a personal calling that's as unique as a fingerprint
and that the best way to succeed is to discover
what you love and then find a way to offer it to others
in the form of service, working hard, and also allowing
the energy of the universe to lead you.

Oprah Winfrey

Closing Thoughts

YOU did it! If you have completed this 31-day journey, you have changed your life in a special way. I'm so proud of you and you should be SO proud of you, too! I'm sure this journal and the questions presented were not always easy, but you pushed through. You are a VIP!

I absolutely enjoyed creating this journal with you in my every thought and key stroke. These are steps that I have taken over the years to achieve my goals and walk in JOY and purpose. These are also questions I have asked of others who have sought my humble advice when they were facing life challenges. I have also utilized and recommended each of the steps to those looking to create something beautiful in life and just needed a little boost of encouragement.

Know that I wrote this journal with the intention of touching your heart and sparking a new fire in you to seek your dreams unconditionally. Having clarity helps you flow in the gifts you were created to share

with the world. You have a responsibility to shine bright in your gifts and talents, never hold back, and play your life full out.

My prayer is that this Endless JOY Journal helps you gain that clarity; that it moves you a step closer to a life filled with JOY and that it gives you courage and confidence to DREAM BIG and THRIVE in JOY!

It would be my true pleasure to work with you some day in gaining clarity and creating a DREAM Plan for your joyous life. A life where you operate with purpose, in purpose, and on purpose!

Thank you for trusting me to help you navigate this journey!

With Sisterly LOVE,

31 Days to Actualize Your Dream and Thrive

About the Author

Hello, I am TeQuita A. White-Muhammed, wife, mother to the wonderful 3Ts (Terranesha, Telleyana, and Tashlyn), and loving supporter to my family and friends.

I love being the Senior Business Analyst Consultant and Chief Transformation Officer of 3T Envisage Consultancy LLC, based in Dallas, Texas. Our firm is a Professional Management Services organization dedicated to strategic transformation, innovation, and growth.

I am also the founder of the She's VIP Network, a group dedicated to presenting workshops and seminars focused on bridging the six-figure market place gap for professional women throughout the world.

I am dedicated to serving God and humanity with my gifts and talents. Each day I am chanced with working with aha-mazing individuals and organizations; it's a true delight to my spirit. I am NOT a life coach, therapist, or healer. I am an inspirational speaker, mentor, business owner, and with this journal a published author!

My motto is "Champion your ideas, Actualize your Dreams, and Thrive in JOY!!"

Learn more about my organization 3T Envisage Consultancy LLC by visiting online at:
www.TransformWithTequita.com

How to Share this Journal

We would love it if you'd share your journal on all of your social media channels. Post a picture of what you're working through in your 31 Day Endless JOY Journal. Use the #EndlessJOYJournal on all your posts so we can create a tribe of JOY-filled VIPs that inspire others to thrive in infinite joy!

#EndlessJOYJournal
Website: www.endlessjoyjournal.com
Instagram: @EndlessJOYJournal
Author Website: www.TransformWithTequita.com

Thank you for entrusting me on your

Endless Joy Journey!

TAWM

31 Days to Actualize Your Dream and Thrive

CPSIA information can be obtained
at www.ICGtesting.com
Printed in the USA
FSHW010201040619
58671FS

9 780578 495705